Celebrations in My World

Diwali

Crabtree Publishing Company

www.crabtreebooks.com

Crabtree Publishing Company

www.crabtreebooks.com

Author: Kate Torpie
Coordinating editor: Chester Fisher
Series editor: Susan Labella
Project manager: Santosh Vasudevan (Q2AMEDIA)
Art direction: Dibakar Acharjee (Q2AMEDIA)
Cover design: Ranjan Singh (Q2AMEDIA)
Design: Neha Gupta (Q2AMEDIA)
Photo research: Sejal Sehgal Wani (Q2AMEDIA)
Editor: Kelley MacAulay
Copy editor: Adrianna Morganelli
Proofreader: Crystal Sikkens
Project editor: Robert Walker
Production coordinator: Katherine Berti
Font management: Mike Golka
Prepress technicians: Samara Parent, Ken Wright

Photographs:
Cover: IP-Zero02/IndiaPicture, Helen Johnson/ Flickr (background); Title page: Photos India/ Photolibrary; P4: Photos India/Photolibrary; P5: thefinalmiracle/Istockphoto; P6: Keith Naylor/ Shutterstock; P9: Helene Rogers/Art Directors & Trip; P10: Barrie Watts/Alamy; P12: Photos India/ Photolibrary; P13: Photos India/Photolibrary; P14: Hill Street Studios/Jupiter Images; P15: Photolibrary; P17: IP-Green/IndiaPicture; P18: Jupiter Images; P19: Sunil281/Dreamstime; P20: Dinodia Photo Library/Jupiter Images (top); P20: Archana Bhartia/ BigStockPhoto (bottom); P21: Mohammed Yousuf/ The Hindu Images; P22: Dinodia Images/Alamy; P23: Graham Oliver/Alamy; P24: Jeremy Hoare/ Alamy; P25: S. Subramanium/The Hindu Images; P26: World Religions Photo Library/Alamy; P27: Bjorn Svensson/Alamy; P28: Dinodia Photo Library/Jupiter Images; P29: Photofusion Picture Library/Alamy; P30: K Murali Kumar/The Hindu Images; P31: IP-Green/IndiaPicture

Illustrations:
Q2A Media Art Bank: P7, 8, 11, 16

Library and Archives Canada Cataloguing in Publication

Torpie, Kate, 1974-
    Diwali / Kate Torpie.

(Celebrations in my world)
Includes index.
ISBN 978-0-7787-4282-1 (bound).--ISBN 978-0-7787-4300-2 (pbk.)

    1. Divali--Juvenile literature. I. Title. II. Series.

BL1239.82.D58T67 2008   j294.5'36   C2008-904106-2

Library of Congress Cataloging-in-Publication Data

Torpie, Kate, 1974-
    Diwali / Kate Torpie.
        p. cm. -- (Celebrations in my world)
    Includes index.
    ISBN-13: 978-0-7787-4300-2 (pbk. : alk. paper)
    ISBN-10: 0-7787-4300-4 (pbk. : alk. paper)
    ISBN-13: 978-0-7787-4282-1 (reinforced library binding : alk. paper)
    ISBN-10: 0-7787-4282-2 (reinforced library binding : alk. paper)
    1. Divali--Juvenile literature. I. Title.

BL1239.82.D58T67 2008
294.5'36--dc22
                                          2008028868

Crabtree Publishing Company

www.crabtreebooks.com   1-800-387-7650

Printed in the USA/052013/IB20130408

Published in Canada
Crabtree Publishing
616 Welland Ave.
St. Catharines, ON
L2M 5V6

Published in the United States
Crabtree Publishing
PMB 59051
350 Fifth Avenue, 59th Floor
New York, New York 10118

Published in the United Kingdom
Crabtree Publishing
Maritime House
Basin Road North, Hove
BN41 1WR

Published in Australia
Crabtree Publishing
3 Charles Street
Coburg North
VIC, 3058

Contents

What is Diwali?

Diwali is a five-day **Hindu** holiday. Hinduism is a religion practiced all over the world. Many people in India are Hindu. Diwali is one of Hinduism's most important holidays. Hindu children look forward to Diwali all year long.

- The word Diwali means "row of lights." This girl holds *diyas*, or clay lamps. They are lit during Diwali.

DID YOU KNOW?

Hinduism is the world's third-most popular religion. Followers believe in Brahman, a soul that connects all living creatures. Brahman is in flowers, in people, and even in insects.

Bright lights and sparkles are everywhere during Diwali! Brightly colored fireworks explode overhead on all five nights of the holiday.

5

What is Hinduism?

Hindus have fun during Diwali, but they also honor their **beliefs**. Hindus believe that there are many gods, not just one.

- Ganesha (right) is the name of a Hindu god. In a Hindu legend, his head was accidentally switched with the head of an elephant! Now, his large ears are said to hear all prayers.

DID YOU KNOW?

Lakshmi is a beautiful Hindu goddess. She is the bringer of wealth and luck. She is honored during Diwali.

Diwali celebrates a god named **Rama** and his wife, **Sita**. Rama was thrown out of his kingdom. While he was away, a **demon** captured his wife! Rama fought the demon and won back his wife and kingdom. Diwali celebrates this victory.

After defeating the demon, Rama and Sita (center and left) returned to ruling their kingdom.

Rama's Victory

During Diwali, people light diyas and fireworks to honor Rama's victory. His victory was one of goodness against evil and light over dark.

*The monkeys in the picture above are soldiers. **Hanuman** is the Hindu god of monkeys. According to legend, his monkey army helped Rama win his battle.*

Hindu people also believe that everyone gets to live more than one life. After death, a person is **reborn** in a different form. If you were good in your last life, your new life will be a good one as a reward. Diwali is a time for people to remember that good triumphs over evil.

Rama fought a fierce battle against many strong demons!

Diwali Stories

Diwali lasts for five fun-filled days and nights. Each day honors a Hindu legend. These legends each teach an important lesson.

● On each night of Diwali, bright lights shine to remind people that light wins over darkness.

DID YOU KNOW?

According to legend, the god Hanuman would light his long monkey tail and thrash it around the demon's city.

One Hindu legend is about a god named **Krishna** who saved a village. A storm was flooding the village. Using just a fingertip, however, Krishna moved an entire mountain to stop the flood and protect the village. He held the mountain over the village like an umbrella!

The story of Krishna reminds people that the gods love them and the people must be thankful.

Diwali Decorations

Families decorate their homes for Diwali with beautiful lights and colors. Many begin decorating before Diwali even starts—they can't wait!

● Candlelight shines in houses on each night of Diwali.

DID YOU KNOW?

Rangolis *are designs that people finger-paint on the floor using rice powder and moist, colored chalk.*

A *rangoli* is a traditional Indian craft. It welcomes the beautiful goddess Lakshmi. It can be painted on the floor of a home or business. Children are encouraged to make creative crafts for Diwali decorations.

Diwali Dancing

Diwali celebrations are like big parties! There is music and traditional dancing. *Garba* is a modern Indian dance. At many Diwali parties, there are *garba* competitions.

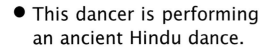

• This dancer is performing an ancient Hindu dance.

DID YOU KNOW?

Garba *is also very popular in the United States. Some colleges have* garba *dance team competitions.*

These children are dressed to dance out a Hindu legend.

Harvest Festival

Diwali is always celebrated in October or November—around the same time that food crops, such as rice, are picked.

● *Poha* is a breakfast dish. It is made with the rice that has just been gathered.

DID YOU KNOW?

Right after Diwali, farmers are back to work. It is time to replant all the empty fields.

Farmers refer to the time of gathering crops as the **harvest**. They take the time to thank Lakshmi during Diwali. They know they must be grateful for a good crop.

All year long, farmers work hard to plant seeds and keep crops healthy.

Diwali Desserts

Holidays such as Diwali are a time for eating great food. Families gather together to make delicious meals for guests. Friends and neighbors give children many kinds of tasty sweets.

On the second day of Diwali, guests arrive early for a traditional breakfast.

DID YOU KNOW?

Families have their own secret recipes for Diwali sweets. Everyone shares their special treats but not their recipes!

Chocolate *Barfi*

Follow this recipe to make your own Diwali treat!

Ingredients

3 lbs ricotta cheese

4 ounces unsalted butter

$\frac{1}{2}$ cup of cocoa powder

$2\frac{1}{2}$ cups sugar

$2\frac{1}{2}$ cups non-fat powdered milk

$1\frac{1}{2}$ cups coarsely crushed almond

2 teaspoons crushed cardamom

Cook the ricotta cheese and butter on low to medium heat. Keep it half covered, stirring often to avoid burning. After about a half hour, stir in the cocoa, sugar and dry milk. Cook, while stirring, until the ricotta is of dry consistency, like paste that can be easily spread (10 to 15 minutes).

Mix in the almonds and crushed cardamom. Spread on a nonstick 12"x18" cookie sheet, about $\frac{1}{3}$-inch thick. Pat gently with wax paper or spatula to make it even. Cut into squares or diamond shapes when cool.

Diwali Duds

During Diwali, friends, family, and neighbors go visiting one another. They gather together for celebrations. Everyone wears their best clothing to these events. Wearing nice clothing honors the host of the gathering and the celebration itself!

- Boys may dress up in a *dhoti kurta* like this one. Underneath, they wear pants called *churidar*. Boys are very comfortable in these outfits!

DID YOU KNOW?

This picture shows mendhi *tattoos made from henna ink. People draw on these designs for parties. The ink lasts for several days.*

A *choli* is a short shirt that shows off your belly.

Indian girls usually wear more than one of these bracelets, which are called bangles.

This long skirt is known as a *ghagra*.

These bells are called *ghungroos*. They jingle when girls dance or walk!

21

Diwali Abroad

Diwali is celebrated by Hindus all over the world. People in different parts of the world celebrate Diwali in different ways. These pages show some Diwali celebrations from around the world.

● In Japan, Hindus lighten the night with paper lanterns. They even hang them from trees.

DID YOU KNOW?

One religious group, called the Jains, celebrate Diwali in a strictly religious way. They even fast, or stop eating, for three days! They offer their suffering to their gods.

Hindus who live in Great Britain also celebrate Diwali. Just like Hindus in India, these people prepare for the holiday by cleaning their homes, wearing new clothes, and decorating with bright lights. They visit their temple to worship Lakshmi, the goddess of wealth, and hang brightly lit lamps in honor of the holiday.

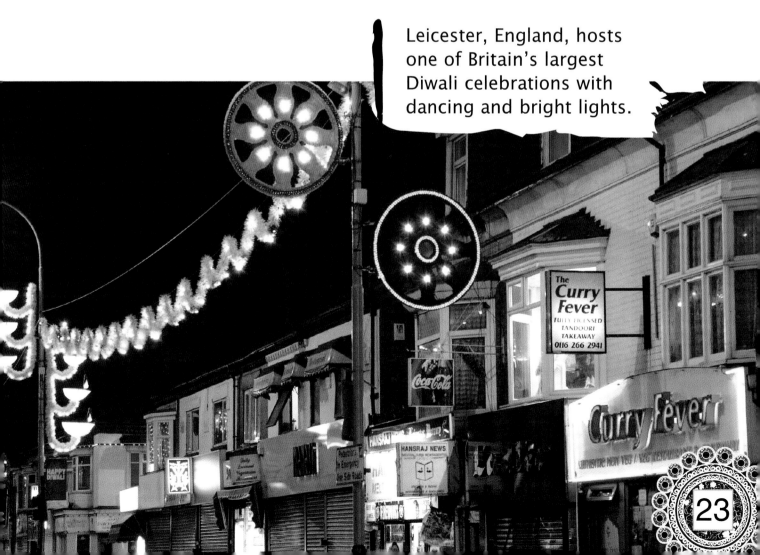

Leicester, England, hosts one of Britain's largest Diwali celebrations with dancing and bright lights.

Kids Love Diwali!

All year long, kids look forward to Diwali. Why wouldn't they? With five days of parties, presents, and sweets, what could be better?

● Young people dance to honor legends that are remembered during Diwali.

DID YOU KNOW?

Playing cards is very popular during Diwali. According to a Hindu legend, people who do not play card games during Diwali will be born as donkeys in their next lives!

Children hold sparklers as the
night sky fills with bright colors.

Children especially look forward
to the fifth day of Diwali. This day
honors the love between sisters
and brothers. They give each other
gifts and are not allowed to fight.

Diwali Symbols

Symbols are part of many Diwali traditions. A **symbol** is something that stands for something else.

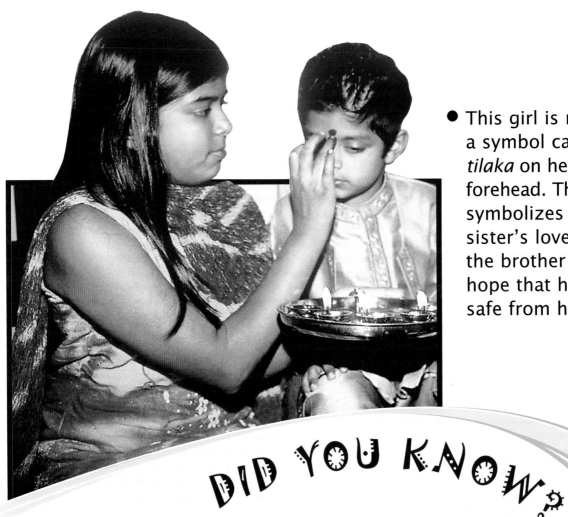

● This girl is marking a symbol called a *tilaka* on her brother's forehead. The *tilaka* symbolizes the sister's love for the brother and her hope that he stays safe from harm.

DID YOU KNOW?

*A hill of sweets is left outside a temple before a ceremony. After the ceremony, the sweets become **prashad**, or gifts from the gods. Children may eat the sweets!*

Many Hindus celebrate Diwali by taking a trip to the Yamuna River. Bathing together symbolizes the families' hopes that they will know each other in their next lives.

Prayer

While Diwali is five days of fun celebrations, it is also a religious holiday. During Diwali, Hindus remember to thank their gods and show them respect. They thank the gods by praying.

- Families pray together. Statues of gods are included on **altars**. The family prays to the statues and offers gifts of thanks.

During Diwali, businesspeople bring gifts to temples. The gifts are to thank Lakshmi for a good year and to ask her for another.

DID YOU KNOW?

A little statue of Lakshmi in her hatri, or house, is a common decoration. People leave candies for her and give her jewelry, such as necklaces.

29

Giving Gifts

Children receive little presents on each day of Diwali. The fourth day of the holiday is devoted entirely to giving gifts. Friends and family get gifts—so do mail carriers, bakers, and even shopkeepers.

● Some people may buy jewelry as gifts.

DID YOU KNOW?

Diwali only lasts for five days and it is not a national holiday. In some parts of India, though, businesses and schools are closed for two weeks at the time of Diwali.

On the day of giving gifts, it is a tradition that you have a gift for every special person in your life.

Glossary

altar A place on which gifts or sacrifices to a god are made

belief Traditional value believed to be true

demon An evil being

Diwali A five-day Hindu religious celebration

Hanuman The Hindu god of monkeys

harvest The time of year when crops are picked and sold in the market

Hindu A person who follows Hinduism

Krishna A god who saved a village

Lakshmi A Hindu goddess of wealth

prashad Sweets that are eaten as gifts of god

Rama A god whose victory over demons marks the beginning of Diwali

reborn To be born again after dying

Sita The wife of Rama

symbol Something that stands for something else

Index